Rambling Arou Rossendale

Waterfoot

Peter and Susan Lord

01413007

All maps based on the Ordnance Survey Map, by permission of the controller of Her Majesty's Stationery Office, crown copyright reserved.

Published by Countryside Publications Limited, School Lane, Brinscall, Chorley, Lancashire.
Text © Peter and Susan Lord, 1985.
ISBN 0 86157 170 3

Contents

Master Map 4

Foreword 5

Making a Pouch 7

Making Gaiters 8

Choose your Walk   Check List 9
carefully . . .

Walk 1: Rawtenstall - Irwell Vale 10
Walk 2: Helm Shore - Stubbins 13
Walk 3: Haslingden - Crawshawbooth 15
Walk 4: Crawshawbooth - Whitewellbottom - Newchurch 19
Walk 5: Stacksteads - Bacup 22
Walk 6: Bacup - Todmorden 25
Walk 7: Stacksteads - Rochdale 30
Walk 8: Ironbridge - Cowpe - Lench 33
Walk 9: Waterfoot - Lench - Rawtenstall 35
Walk 10: Seat Naze Stroll 37
The Country Code 40

*Footpaths may
become a little
damp . . .*

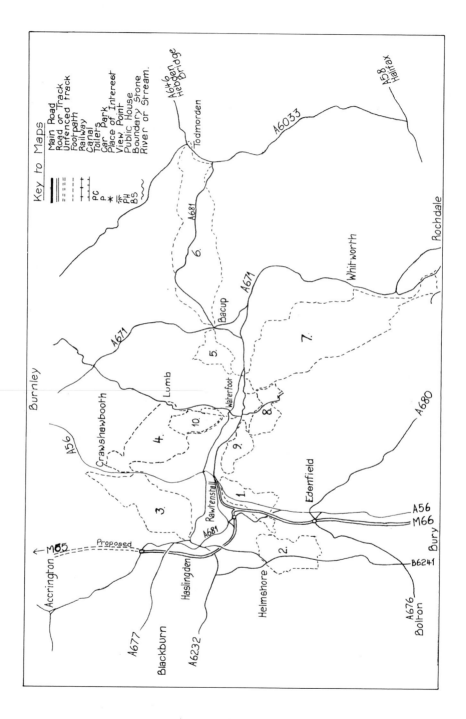

Foreword

We have been rambling for several years in Rossendale and we never tire of the beautiful views in and around the valley. Indeed, there are many paths that we still have not ventured along.

We decided to write this book so we could share, with others, the pleasure of this local free pastime. All the rambles are circular, the longer ones giving you the option of doing half the walk and catching the bus home or to your car. We advise you to check on the bus times though.

The walks use rights of way as shown on the Ordnance Survey Maps and it is useful to take one with you, although not essential.

The majority of paths are little used and so the quality underfoot is often poor, but we feel it is all the better! Also, occasionally, the paths are not very evident but don't be afraid to proceed if you are fairly sure. Remember, a courteous apology, followed by a request for the direction of the correct path, can do no harm.

Unfortunately one or two of the paths have been blocked by wire and fencing (presumably the owner is unaware of the existence of the right of way); however, clamber over carefully and please observe the Country Code.

Remember, walking is free and if you are wise with your choice and lucky with the weather it should be a leisurely and enjoyable pastime.

HANDY HINTS

Common sense is the key factor to enjoying a good day's rambling, but a little bit of planning and organization is a great help.

Firstly choose your walk carefully; consider the members of your group and include them in the choice. When planning the rambles, we feel it is better to do a circular walk thus omitting the need for public transport.

Secondly, if the weather has been particularly wet over the last few days, bear that in mind too because the paths are little used and can be very soggy underfoot.

FOOTWEAR. We both have sturdy leather walking boots and can honestly say we have never had any foot trouble. However I am not saying they are essential on our walks. A pair of strong shoes or trainers (Not pumps, they have too soft undersoles) are equally as good if you do not mind getting wet feet, or very muddy shoes at least! Wellingtons are useful, especially for children and in winter, but remember socks have a habit of walking off and wellies can be cold.

CLOTHING. In summer shorts, T-shirt, a thin jumper and a waterproof cagoule are adequate. A cagoule is a necessity; they are cheap, easy to carry and windproof. Anoraks are far too bulky to carry if you get hot; they are also rarely waterproof. In winter, which round here seems endless, long trousers (NOT jeans), two thin jumpers, cagoule, scarf, hat and gloves are bare requirements. One word about waterproof trousers: we don't like them; they are expensive, noisy and rarely fit comfortably. Gaiters are far better. Granted they only come up to your knee, but they are light, easy to wear, cheaper and do not make you hot. **Karrimor,** which is based in Accrington, make a good pair for about £8, but obviously you can pay more. I made ours from an old cagoule. The real beauty of gaiters is that you can wear them all the time and they prevent mud from travelling up your trouser leg, and they wash easily. An item to include is a polythene sheet or bin liner; it is useful to sit on and you can put all your rubbish in after your picnic.

WHAT TO CARRY. A small rucksack can be bought for about £3. We use a canvas one with shoulder straps and one large pocket. It is not waterproof but if it looks like it might rain we put an extra polythene bag inside. A shoulder bag is better than nothing, but please do not take a plastic carrier; the handles always break and you have one hand tied to carrying it. If you are taking children, let them carry their own sandwiches and drink, it is not too heavy and will certainly lighten your own load. A first aid kit comprising plasters, antiseptic cream, paracetamol and insect bite cream is a useful item.

CHILDREN. Believe it or not young children are capable of walking six or seven miles without difficulty . . . providing they are warm, have comfortable footwear and kept interested. Show them the trees, point out and identify flowers. (There are plenty of pocket size handbooks). Do not let children pick flowers; they might be a protected species. With very young children - five to seven - stop often for a little rest, try not to let them run round too much. Often they will run ahead then run back to you, and when you're only half way round they have already walked twice as far! When you stop for your picnic encourage them to sit whilst they eat theirs, play I-spy or another word game so that they do rest occasionally.

The time taken for each of our walks is intended only as a rough guide. We admit to dawdling, we stop often, look at things of interest, and most importantly we savour the views. Don't rush round; you will miss things. Remember, walking is a relaxing hobby if you go at your own pace and do what comes naturally.

LAST WORD. Let someone know whereabouts you are rambling. The Rossendale Valley has its own Fell Rescue Team, and hopefully you will never need them, but even so if you did fail to return then at least your relative or friend would be able to give a rough location.

HOW TO MAKE POUCH OR CAGOULE

NEED: Nylon material (size to be decided). Two pieces of one inch wide elastic (long enough to fit around you waist, including the pouch).

1. Fold your cagoule into a neat compact square, make sure it is not too fat.

2. Measure around its edge (Mine was 10" by 6").

3. Cut two pieces of the nylon material slightly larger and sew them together leaving the top open.

4. Fit a zip.

5. With elastic sew neatly to either side of pouch, at top.

6. Fit buckle.

These pouches are invaluable because you do not have to rummage through your rucksack if it begins to rain.

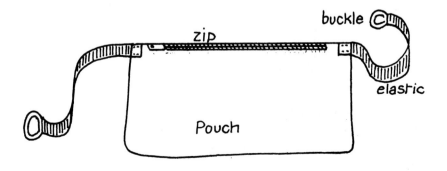

7

How to make a pair of Gaiters.

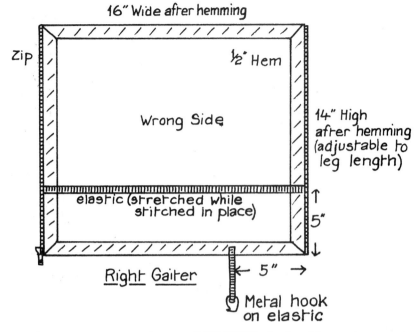

16" Wide after hemming

Zip

½" Hem

Wrong Side

14" High after hemming (adjustable to leg length)

elastic (stretched while stitched in place)

5"

Right Gaiter

← 5" →

Metal hook on elastic

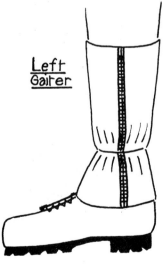

Left Gaiter

YOU NEED: **1.** An old cagoule or some nylon material approx. 17" wide x 15" high. (You can adjust the height by measuring from the ankle to the knee). **2.** Two open-ended zips. Check the length as it varies. **3.** Two pieces of elastic 1" wide x 8" long. Two pieces about 10" long but only ½" wide. Lastly two hooks. The hook from a hook and eye set is all right, but it must be fairly big.

METHOD: **1.** Hem the nylon all the way round (about ½" in). **2.** 5" up from the bottom, place the long elastic and machine in while stretched. **3.** Fit zip. **4.** 5" in along the bottom, sew the short elastic with the hook attached at the end. (I suggest you wear the gaiters with the zips on the outside of the legs because mud can jam the zip). The short elastic needs to be placed approx 5" in away from each zip. The hook is hooked over the furthest piece of lace on your boot or shoe and helps to keep the gaiter in place.

CHECK LIST

1. Select walk, read commentary through. Useful (but not essential) to get the Ordnance Survey Map. Available from the library.

Place the book, open at correct page, in a clear plastic bag.

2. Pack rucksack. (a) Bin liner . . . (b) Packed lunch or tea . . . (c) Drink. Flasks are nice in winter. Use a litre plastic bottle and make up a cordial drink for the children. Cans of pop finish too quickly . . . (d) An extra jumper . . . (e) First aid kit.

3. Clothing. If you're driving to the start of the ramble, leave a jumper off and re-dress as you set off. Always have your gaiters on; muddy areas occur unexpectedly!

4. Leave word with someone.

5. Take camera, binoculars, spotters handbook and small change.

Better to use non-slip footwear.

RAWTENSTALL - IRWELL VALE

6 miles - 4 hrs.

We are never out of sight of those rolling hills at any place in Rossendale. Hills challenge those who are want to climb to their summits, but the aim of this walk is to allow the rambler the views without exertion and afterwards to return by the riverside.

1. Your starting point is just off the large traffic island at Rawtenstall. We suggest you park just off the old Edenfield Road, by the telephone exchange, which is on Newhallhey Road. Commence walking by crossing the old road and climb the steep road opposite, passing the back of Asda Superstore (Hall Carr Road). Ascend through the housing estate which route diminishes to a

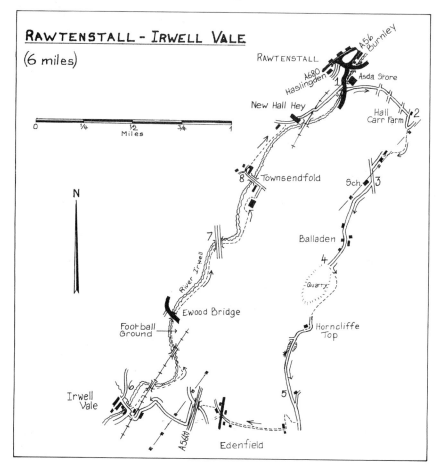

track to Hall Carr Farm. If you turn around at this point to view the scenery over Rawtenstall you will be amply rewarded. Cribden Hill is immediately in front of you and on its lower slopes can be seen Ski Rossendale, one of the longest artificial ski runs in the country. The transmitting aerials to the north are on Hameldon Hill, where Radio Lancashire joins the airwaves.

2. Bear right at Hall Carr Farm on a more gentle incline, and as the track turns sharply left take the stile on the right into open country. The path continues slightly uphill towards a gate, following a broken stone wall on your left. There is a high wooden stile to the right of the gate, after which you continue downhill to a stile and gate half way along the lower fence. Go through the gap in the stone slab wall and follow the pylons to a gate in the corner of the field, then to a track through a farm.

3. At the tarmac road turn left up-hill and bear right as you pass the primary school. Continue along here past several houses on your right; at the end you will see a steep incline down to a river. It is here where a new house slid a number of yards after a severe storm in the 1970s. Continue through the hamlet of Balladen and climb the rough track to a disused quarry. The path takes the left course at the high fence, following a wall on your left to a stile.

4. Care is needed here as the ground has been rather churned by heavy vehicles, but a track is to the right and forward, climbing slightly. A distinct, although now green, track will soon become apparent; it may be rather wet and follows the top of the quarry. A crater blocks the track and the route is by a path on the left side. The table-like hill directly in front of you is Musbury Tor, a plateau with steep escarpments on three sides. The track is rather overgrown beyond the old rusty gate, but press on, choosing your steps carefully, to the large white-washed farmhouse built in 1861. Cross the very large parking area and continue down the lane to a white-gate-stile. Soon there is a track on the right, but you go straight on through a cutting. Suddenly the view opens away on your right, making your effort worthwhile! In the distance, eastwards, is Haslingden and Helmshore, while southwards is Ramsbottom, with Holcombe Tower beyond. This is the Vale of Irwell traversed by the new Edenfield to Rawtenstall by-pass. Continue along the track through the gate, and on your left is a slope which is ideal for a picnic, with the view set out before you.

5. Carry on southwards to pass below the house on the hilltop, and take the stile on the right. Then follow the path down steeply to the track through a stile by a gate to the farm. The farm lane takes you to a cattle grid and on to the main road. Cross this road to a cobbled road opposite. After passing a farm on the left there is a narrow path. Turn left and follow it down to the main Edenfield-Haslingden road. Cross this and go under the by-pass, turning left immediately up Hardsough Lane. This lane bends right past Grange House on the left and down to a level crossing in Irwell Vale. Cross the track and go forward to the bridge.

6. Your path is along the river bank to the right where, just before the bridge, there is a gap in the railings. You may wish to proceed to admire the olde worlde terraced cottages just beyond the bridge. Follow the river bank under the railway bridge. A little further the path climbs gradually to a fence, but drops sharply back to the river and a stile alongside. Another railway bridge is soon passed and the path opens on to Ewood Bridge Football Club Ground. Keep to the bank and climb the steps to the road. After crossing, more steps bring you back to the river again.

The next bridge you meet passes under the by-pass, and heralds a gentle stroll to Rawtenstall outskirts, beginning with **K-Steels** new factory. The right of way follows down the river side of the building and across to the main gate. Continue along the approach road and turn left at the junction.

8. This hamlet is Townsendfold, where a train once crashed through the leve-crossing gate and hit a car. After the river is crossed you pass a house called **The Holme.** Go right after this building and return to the river bank. Before long you pass a farm building. A stile, which is merely a gap in the wall, is your exit. Go right and under the arch in the mill wall. After a level crossing is Newhallhey Road . . . from where your walk began.

Irwell near Chatterton

HELMSHORE - STUBBINS

5 miles - 3 hrs.

This is a ramble which climbs gradually to a vantage point over the Vale of the River Irwell, and then descends by a babbling brook and returns by the meandering river.

1. There is limited parking space opposite the Memorial Gardens at Helmshore, and the walk begins by following Sunnybank Road under the bridge and past the site of a large cotton mill. At the fork go left along the cobbled track, and at the junction cross and enter the field opposite by the iron kissing-gate.

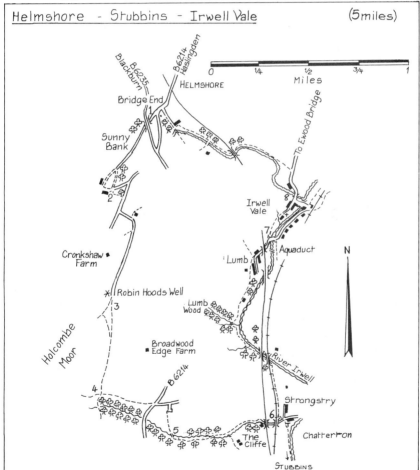

Helmshore - Stubbins - Irwell Vale   (5miles)

2. Your path goes left and ascends, passing a telegraph pole, to go on to the right of a little copse. Arriving at the copse, you will see a second kissing-gate and you turn right here, taking the left track sign-posted to Robin Hoods Well (Moor Road). The well will be seen on your right when you are nearing the very top of this wet track. Turn and admire the view.

3. Continue through the metal gate and follow the wall on your left. Walk at the higher level to avoid wetness underfoot and to take in the view over the valley. On a clear day you can see down to Edenfield, Bury and beyond.

4. Your path turns left through the metal gate just before a copse which belongs to the National Trust. The track descends to the B6214, the Blackburn-Bury turn-pike road built by "Blind" Jack Metcalfe of Knaresborough from 1788 onwards. Take the farm track opposite, but turn first right and enter the field by the gate on the right. The right of way follows the fence down towards the little valley, over a wooden stile, then by a wall down to a stone slab bridge. Be careful here, it was rather slippy when we crossed it!

5. This next section is ideal for picnics. The path follows the river and crosses it again. At the stile and bridge keep forward with the stream on your right. A track takes you past a farm and under two railway bridges to arrive at the hamlet of Stongstry. A pleasant walk to Stubbins, by the riverside, beings on your right if you have time. An interesting point about Chatterton, which is a little village just across the river, is that here on 26th April 1826 five men and five women were shot dead by the cavalry, following riots by Luddites who had rampaged through Accrington and Haslingden wrecking mill property, fearing for their livelihood because of the advent of powered looms.

River Irwell

6. The return journey takes a path from Strongstry by the railway, starting opposite the telephone box. Follow the path under the two railway bridges as they cross the River Irwell. The next stretch can be very wet and care is needed at several points, but the walk is interesting. The path follows the river bank through the glade. To cross a stream you will need to ascend a little. The path climbs by a fence to the top of the escarpment and turns left to enter a side valley and crosses two streams. Climb again and cross the fence near a barn. A track leads you to a road at Lumb and this takes you under a railway arch.

7. Leave the road before the river bridge by a gap in the wall on the left. Continue by the river, taking as dry a route as possible. By a garden wall there is a little stone slab bridge crossing a tiny beck and the path follows the wall to a wooden stile, from where your way later joins a lane by the Methodist Chapel in Irwell Vale village. Take the main street, a rather traditional street of mill cottages built in 1833.

8. Cross the bridge at the end of the street and follow the road to take a stile by the first gate on the left. The path leaves the road and continues to a stile near the river. Continue under the railway viaduct and past the bridge to a white house. Take the wooden-gate stile by the cottages and follow the lane away from the river, by a little park, back to your starting point.

Bottom left: River Irwell, Chatterton.

WALK 3

HASLINGDEN - CRAWSHAWBOOTH

6½ miles - 5 hrs.

This walk surrounds Cribden Hill, which separates Haslingden from Crawshawbooth. There is a short section of open moorland which should put no one off as it is very easy to negotiate. Towards the end there are splendid views over Rawtenstall. An extension to 13 miles by also doing Walk 4 will provide a full day's ramble if so desired.

1. The start is from the car park off Higher Deardengate, behind Haslingden library. At the head of Higher Deardengate cross Bury Road and ascend Church Street, passing St. James' Church and turning left onto High Street and then right along Higher Lane. Keep forward at the sharp bend to pass several stables and the rear of Slate Farm, then turn left at the gulley. It can be very wet along this stretch so extra care is needed.

HASLINGDEN - CRAWSHAWBOOTH

(6½ miles)

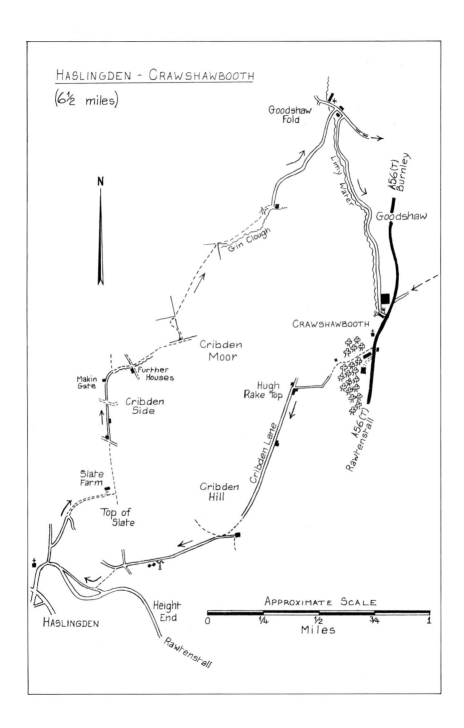

Goodshaw
Fold

N

Limy Water

A56(T)
Burnley

Goodshaw

Gin Clough

CRAWSHAWBOOTH

Cribden
Moor

Makin
Gate

Further
Houses

Hugh
Rake Top

Cribden
Side

Cribden Lane

A56(T)
Rawtenstall

Slate
Farm

Cribden
Hill

Top of
Slate

Height
End

HASLINGDEN

Rawtenstall

APPROXIMATE SCALE

| 0 | ¼ | ½ | ¾ | 1 |

Miles

2. Cross the road to the tip and pass Green House Farm and later Makin Gate Farm, where your path goes right of the building and curves to the right. Cross a gate to a path ascending to a little copse to Further Houses. Follow the stream up the Shallow valley past a crag and through a gate ahead. Cross the drain channel and keep by the wall on your left. On nearing the summit your path turns left after a wall curves away from the one you have been following. Keeping this second wall on your left you will find a stile taking you to the far side, but only for a short while as you cross back at the corner of the field.

3. The next section over the horizon is not distinct, but with your back to the stile you should walk in the direction of 10 o'clock, heading for a white house in the distant trees below the transmitting aerials. You will soon see a stile in the corner of the field, and, after crossing it, turn right, keeping by the wall and so through a stile in a fence. Now you follow a gradually emerging track which bears left around the hillside before you. There is a wooden bridge before the farmhouse at the head of the clough.

The farm lane goes away left of the farm and takes you into Goodshaw Fold, where if you go left a little distance the spring known as the Spewing Duck can be seen, and cool refreshment taken.

4. Turn to retrace your steps up the road as far as the next lane on the right beyond that by which you arrived. (Those who are extending the walk should

Near Hawkshaw

not turn here, but continue up the road, cross the A56 and take Hamer Avenue opposite, bearing right and turning left up a path behind the new bungalows. This path climbs to the old road, and Goodshaw Old Chapel, point 2 of Walk 4, can be seen to your right).

To continue **this** walk turn right and follow the river Limy Water along Stoneholme Lane into Crawshawbooth. Watch for the picturesque Friend's Meeting House set in a lovely garden. Turn left here to enter the town. Toilets are available opposite.

5. Go down the main road, taking the left pavement as it is not continuous on the right. Pass the church and continue as far as the bend at the top of the rise. Your path is opposite, along the rear of the row of cottages just before Swinshaw Hall gates. This path is called Hugh Rake and is a steep, narrow ancient track presenting a very stiff climb through the trees to bring you out of the valley. Do not rush!

Continue along the farm track to Hugh Rake Top and turn left around the back of the barns. Keep forward along this high level lane past another farmhouse and through a gate. Along this stretch are spectacular views over Rawtenstall, especially in the evening when street lights are illuminated.

Cross a very sturdy stile and keep on this level above Cribden End Farm and watch for the stile in the wall on your left by a metal pole.

6. Take this stile and turn right down the long lane heading for the TV mast. Keep forward where the tracks cross and take the stile on the left where a fence begins. The path descends the field to a stile giving access to Rock Hall Lane. Turn right and follow this lane down to Church Street and back to your starting point in Haslingden.

Sit and relax now and then.

WALK 4
CRAWSHAWBOOTH - LUMB - WHITEWELLBOTTOM - NEWCHURCH

$7\frac{1}{2}$ miles - 6 hrs.

Here we have a slightly longer walk, but as there is very little climbing it is quite easy.

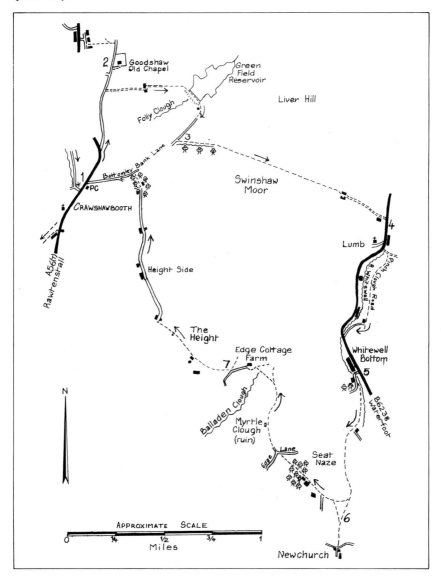

We visit an ancient monument and cross the moors by a path once used by early Baptists each Sunday from 1760 when there were few chapels in existence. The return journey has views over Waterfoot and Rawtenstall.

The start is at the centre of Crawshawbooth. You should try to find suitable side road parking as the A56 is very busy. Public toilets are available near the zebra-crossing.

This walk may be done in conjunction with Walk 3, making the total length about 13 miles, and while the route may be joined at any point on its circuit it is recommended that you begin in Haslingden (See Walk 3).

1. The walk starts by a steady climb up the main road for a short distance and then turning right along Goodshaw Lane as far as Goodshaw Chapel. This building set in its own tranquil graveyard is one of the oldest Baptist chapels in the country. Built in 1760, it has recently been renovated by the Department of the Environment. Sadly there is only one service held here each year, on the first Sunday in July, when the music is provided by a small string orchestra. The congregations of the 18th Century would walk miles each week, some over Swinshaw Moor from Lumb, which is where you are now destined.

2. On leaving the chapel you should take a farm track through a gate a little way down the lane. This will bring you to some farm buildings where the track bends left then right, becoming a mere path heading for the dam of Greenfield Reservoir. Follow the track across the dam and round to the right where it becomes a walled lane.

3. Soon after a gate across the lane you should look for a recess in the wall on your left, for here is your path via a stile alongside a tree-lined ditch. This is the start of a long, straight and distinct path over the moor, involving very little ascent. After several stiles you will descend to go between farm buildings where a track takes you to the road at Lumb.

4. Cross the road and turn right to the bend where a footpath sign indicates your route over the River Whitewell, and then, bearing right, follow a sturdy fence on your right.

This is Pinch Clough Road, now only a grass path but once the only line of transport high above the valley bottom. At the farm turn right to descend to the road, where you should cross, turn left and follow past the Post Office at Whitewell Bottom.

5. Soon after Lambert Howarth's shoe factory a sign showing a public footpath along a street to cross the river indicates the course you should take. Climb the track past the cottages on the right, then turn onto a path on the left where the concrete surface begins. Take great care along here as there is a sheer drop to the river on the left; the bonus of this elevated position is the view up and down the valley.

The path descends to some cottages after passing a mill chimney once fed by a tunnel from a boiler far below. At the cottages do not be tempted to descend the cobbled lane but follow the leafy path hugging the hillside around some ruins to a level path above several craters, no doubt caused by mining collapses. I have heard of a mine tunnel nearby that was open at both ends; the far end was near Crawshawbooth!

Eventually a gate is reached giving access to a green lane above a garden and large house. Soon you arrive at the old turnpike road at Newchurch, once the main valley town and centre of learning.

6. To continue it is best to retrace your steps to the gate where your path climbs to a stile on the left. Turn here onto a walled path which takes you round Seat Naze Hill to a path by a primary school. Head for the woodland in front; this is Heightside House estate, which has been the conference and administration centre of the European Christian Mission. The house contains a conference hall, recording studio and a printing shop.

At the rear of the house your path crosses a cobbled lane to join a terrace walk. A stone stile marks the exit to a field, and a distinct path descends a little and follows a broken wall on your left to a stile and gate. Here is Edge Lane where you go down to the gate ahead. You are again on the open moorland and you should follow a gulley as it bears right and ascends to the head of Balladen Clough. When the path nears Edge Cottage Farm it follows the garden perimeter to join the tarmac drive.

Ratenstall ramble

7. Just outside the gate your path leaves the track where it turns to descend. There is a rather high step to a level path around the hillside to a stile in a fence. Now you descend towards the farmhouse ahead. You will find a gap in a low wall and a narrow wooden gate to your right. Take this gate and follow the wall on your left to a second, similar gate. Here, do not go up or down the track but straight ahead to a stile over a wall and then onward to a gateway. Continue past the stone barn on your left and through a gateway. After two further wooden stiles you follow the green track until it becomes a lane passing Height Side Farm and several other farmhouses.

On nearing Crawshawbooth the lane turns sharply left by a bungalow where there is a pleasant but short footpath starting ahead at the side of a stone garage. Take this path down to the lane where you turn left to descend to the main road at the beginning of this walk.

Those of you who started from Haslingden should turn left to go through the centre of Crawshawbooth and continue reading at Point 5 of Walk 3.

WALK 5   O/S 103
STACKSTEADS - BACUP
$3\frac{3}{4}$ miles - $2\frac{1}{2}$ hrs.

This is suitable for an evening stroll which is fairly short and gentle.

1. Start from the large car park in Stacksteads where there are toilets. The path is opposite the Working Men's Club and takes you up through the trees to Booth Road. Cross to the farm track on the left of the large stone garage and make the gradual ascent past the houses on the left to a deep cutting over which a Tramway once ran from a colliery to Booth Road. At Honey Hole you will feel to be in the heart of the countryside as you follow the track past the farm buildings.

2. Where the track turns left to climb the hillside you should turn off right above a stone barn. The path is green and takes you to a stile by a rusty gate and then a path following the treeline. A wooden stile and a wall with steps gives access to a field, where your path is clearly visible down to a wooden bridge. Pass between the farmhouse and barn and turn left through the gate, passing stables to follow a stoney track up the valley. The climb eases after a broken gate post and the path is via a kissing gate at the corner of the field.

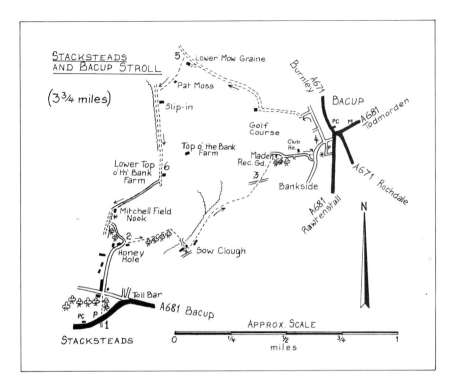

3. Cross directly over the field to a stile, and then between football pitches to arrive by the swings at the Maden Recreation Grounds. Here you may wish to rest or allow the young at heart to exercise on the rings and bars, or perhaps to enjoy a gentle swing. There was a whole line of delightful swingboats and an old-fashioned sweetshop here in the 1960s. Pass through the avenue of trees planted in 1902 to commemorate the coronation of King Edward VII and leave by the main gate. Descend the road past the Golf Clubhouse. Where the road bends to the right go down the steps on your left and turn left to descend to Bacup town centre, passing TV's Juliet Bravo's police station on the right. You may wish to visit the market on Wednesdays and Saturdays, or the Natural History Museum in the former Hare and Hounds Inn on Yorkshire Street. .

4. The return journey begins from Dale Street, so retrace your footsteps up Bankside Lane as far as the police station. Once on Dale Street look for Ross Hill Street and ascend to the track on the right at the top. Follow the tarmac road through the golf course, veering to the right at the stone buildings.

5. Further on, after passing a house on your left at Lower Mow Graine, there is a stile also on the left near a barn. The right of way crosses the field to the lower far corner. Cross two stiles and go to the farm ruins in the distance at

Pat Moss, then follow a shallow gulley to a gate. Turn left at the track, passing Slip in Farm ruins on the left, and continue down a green track with a deep gulley on the right. Further on the stream has escaped onto the track, so it is advisable to cross the broken wall to a higher level in very wet conditions.

6. Cross the stile by a gate and pass another farmhouse at Lower top o'th'Bank, then bear right and follow track, noting views south and west over the wall. Your path goes to the right of a farm at Mitchell Field Nook, then crosses a stream by a little stone bridge on the left. There was once a work house here until late last century. After a descent you may recognise the surroundings from earlier in the walk. Retrace your steps through the cutting down to Booth Road and across it to descend the snickett to the car park.

Scout Bottom

BACUP - TODMORDEN

11 miles - Full days ramble

This is a pleasant full day's walk which straddles the Lancashire-Yorkshire border. There are plenty of views from the hilltops, but you should be prepared for open moorland on the last section where there is no distinct path visible. Do not let this put you off, as there is no possibility of straying far from the designated route. The return journey can be made by Mid-Pennine Link bus; the last bus leaves Todmorden at about 6pm. But check timetable.

1. The walk starts in Bacup centre, where there are several carparks, but I would suggest the one to use is that by the police station above Market Street. You should descend to the round-about, turning left into Burnley Road towards the Post Office. Here you will find toilets.

Go past the toilets on Boston Road (rear of Woolworths), then turn left up Lanehead Lane. Above the third house door on your left is the plaque showing that John Wesley preached here in 1761.

Continue up the hill and follow the road round to the right and pass the cricket ground on your left. As the road beings to descend take a walled lane on your left after Windermere Road. Ascend to Laneside, passing a row of cottages on your left and note the circular walled enclosure beyond, locally known as the Bullring, but which once contained several trees and was no doubt used as a sheep pen. Continue uphill where the track becomes stoney and passes Flowers Farm and the site of the Old Blue Bell.

Eventually the track levels and descends to the A681 where it crosses the county boundary, just beyond the pylons. Turn left and look at the pretty garden after the cottages - it seems a lovely oasis among the moors.

2. Continue up the road but keep straight on where the main road bends right. You are now on Flower Scar Road and this is followed for $1\frac{1}{2}$ miles to Sourhall. Once a pleasant pack horse route, this area is shamefully used as a dumping ground at several points. By a left-hand bend the view opens up to show Stoodley Pike almost $4\frac{1}{2}$ miles away on the horizon directly ahead.

3. You soon join a tarmacadam road taking you down to Sourhall and the Dog and Partridge Inn. Continue straight on, but at the crest of the hill you may find it worthwhile to take the path on the raised verge on the right of the road, in order to see the view to the left over Cliviger Gorge to Bride stones. At the sharp right hand bend take the track down to the stables, after which turn down a long walled grass way. After a stile and gate keep the wall on your right to a second gate, joining the Calderdale Way. The surprise around the next bend is a magnificent view over Centre Vale Park, and you descend through the trees to a road. Turn left down the road, but make a mental note of the old roadway that leads off to your right. This is the start of your homeward journey, but you may wish to tarry a while in the park.

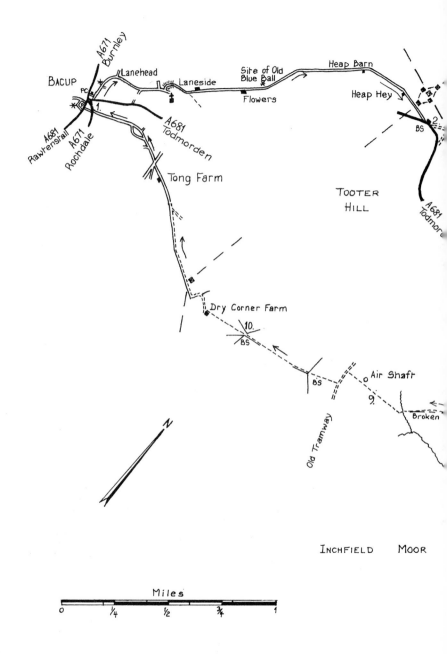

BACUP

A671 Burnley

Lanehead

Laneside

Site of Old Blue Ball

Flowers

Heap Barn

Heap Hey

BS

PC

A681 Rawtenstall

A671 Rochdale

A681 Todmorden

Tong Farm

TOOTER HILL

A681 Todmor

Dry Corner Farm

10.
BS

BS

Air Shaft

9.

Broken

N

Old Tramway

INCHFIELD MOOR

Miles

0   ¼   ½   ¾   1

BACUP - TODMORDEN (11 miles)

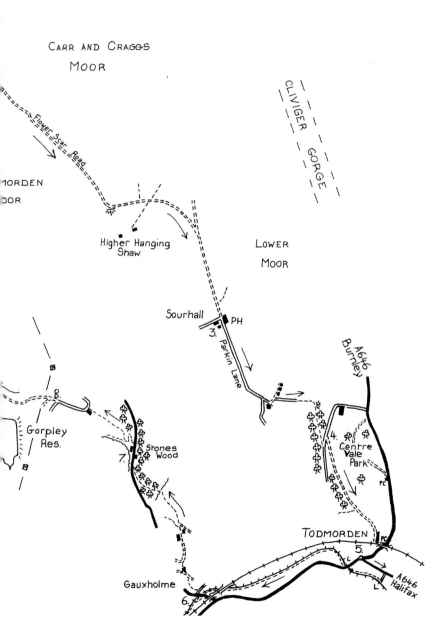

CARR AND CRAGGS MOOR

Flower Scar Road

...ORDEN ...OR

CLIVIGER GORGE

Higher Hanging Shaw

LOWER MOOR

Sourhall PH
3.
Parkin Lane

A646 Burnley

Gorpley Res.
8.
Stones Wood
7.
2.
4.
Centre Vale Park

TODMORDEN
5.
Gauxholme
6.
A646 Halifax

4. The walk home starts from the old roadway, so you may have to retrace your steps. This route affords the best view over Todmorden and misses the main road. The roadway passes above the rooftop level and you descend some steps on your left beside a house. More toilets and the town centre are ahead of you, under the railway viaduct.

5. When you are ready to leave go from the roundabout down Halifax Road (check your time at this point; it is not advisable to attempt the last stretch if dusk is approaching because, as previously mentioned, the path over the moor is not distinct), and turn right at the second road to join the canal by a lock. Follow the towpath to your right which has recently been renovated. Take the narrow tunnel which climbs as it passes under Rochdale Road to a second lock. This is the Rochdale Canal, which has not been navigable for many decades but is a lovely linear park stretching to Hebden Bridge. Cross the canal here and continue along the towpath. Note the incredible brick wall which prevents the railway from sliding down to the earlier line of transport. Eventually you pass under a turreted bridge, carrying the railway to Rochdale. A little further on there is a road bridge, after which you should leave the canal, crossing over this bridge to the other side.

6. Turn right after the bridge, ascending to a green path on the left. Take this path which climbs and bears right round a crag. Do not forget to turn and take in the view behind you. The path soon levels and you begin to descend to a little cottage. The path you should look for passes very closely to the cottage and leads you through a gate into a field. Here you will find a track taking you up to a farm, passing a tiny lodge. Go behind the farm and the path takes you over a little bridge, and then descend through Stones Wood to the road. Here is your last chance to catch a bus home!

7. Cross the road and take an overgrown path on the left past a disused mill with arched windows. The path has a wire fence on your left, then quickly turns right, climbing and twisting to the field at the summit. The path takes you across the field and to the right of a farm. Turn left on a metalled road for a short while.

8. The road bears left, but you should keep straight along a sandy road under pylons and follow on to a bungalow where you bear right, climbing gradually, with the reservoir on your left. When the track ends follow the broken wall which bears round to the left. After a deep valley (which was a little wet when we did the walk) you should turn right to clamber through the grass to a tall thin metal pole put there as a market many years ago.

9. Scan the horizon and you should be able to spot another marker. Keeping the reservoir and the first pole directly behind you, travel due west towards the second pole. Soon you will pass the second marker and an old air shaft. **Go near this at your peril.** Carry straight on keeping both poles and reservoir directly behind you until you come upon a track (once an old tramway). Turn left and continue for twenty yards or so when you will see a large amount of shale. Turn right here and, keeping Stoodley Pike behind you, continue up towards the horizon, where a wall will appear. You are now back in Lancashire, and the right of way crosses the wall where three walls meet.

Now keep the wall on your left and continue ahead. Eventually you will come upon five walls. Cross them, carrying straight on.

10. Soon you will see a TV mast and then a farm. Descend to go to the right of the farm, known as Dry Corner, and onto a farm track, following it to the right. This track leads you to Bacup town centre via Pennine Road.

Todmorden

STACKSTEADS - ROCHDALE

13 miles - Full days ramble

This is a very varied ramble taking in moorland, quarry country and railway track, returning via the old Packhorse route once used to bring cotton to the cottage weaving industry of two centuries ago.

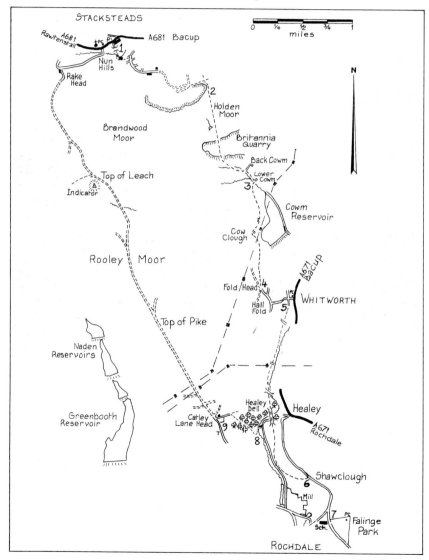

1. There is a suitable carpark on the A681, at Stacksteads, where toilets are available. Cross the road and turn right by the Working Men's Club, following this road past the ford and under the old railway bridge. Your way turns into a narrow path between slab walling. Bear left at the old mill and follow the rear wall until you come to steps leading up to Greens and on up to Cutler Lane. The road narrows to become a mere track up to the quarry, which closed in 1980, and is reputed to have its stone in the foundations of the Eiffel Tower in Paris. At the summit, where the track bends right, your path is to the left and ascends and levels. After a walled bank on the right turn right past the pond and head for a gateway. At the gate carry on in the same direction to follow a shallow valley to a post. Here you must skirt the quarry edge, until the dip is again reached.

2. Your path leads across the open moorland on an ancient track, apparent as a wide depression in the level of the plateau. You should follow this track southwards and soon you will come upon a working quarry. Follow around the edge of this quarry until you can carefully descend into the little valley. The path follows a little river towards Cowm Reservoir. Look out for the crescent-shaped lodge which powered a water wheel for the stone crushing mill at Dules Mouth in the mid-1800s. A grinding wheel would have been used similar to that in front of the Health Centre in Bacup. In 1975 there was a tremendous blaze in quarry-holes above the reservoir, when thousands of tyres burned fiercely, creating a lethal brew of liquid phenol in deep rocky caverns. On July 18th 1975 the thick oily mass burst out of the workings and took over the stream at the head of a clough above Dules Mouth rubbing mill, and thence into the reservoir, filling the valley with a horrid stench. Worse still, the water supply was poisoned and watercarts had to be brought into use; the reservoir has not provided drinking water since. This very expensive reservoir lasted only one hundred years, and it is hoped it will soon be totally drained allowing the valley floor to return to nature.

3. Before a track beings turn right. The track drops into the ruined hamlet of Cowclough, which was quite a community in the 1800s. Cowclough Farm existed in 1759, as a family called Lord lived there, and in 1851 as many as 52 people lived in this bleak hamlet. All had left, however, by 1928, and the whole valley was deserted by 1950. You ascend on this path and keep forward, leaving the reservoir behind, until Fold Head is reached.

4. Here you descend the road to Hall Fold and down to the left. On your right there is the site of an old chapel, now reduced to a few gravestones. Follow the road down past the school and up over the old railway. If you require toilets or ice creams go ahead to the main road at this point.

5. Your path turns right opposite Cowm Park Way South - you are now on the railway - but it has been built on. Go through Massey Croft, passing recently built flats and straight onto the track passing under an old stone bridge. You are now to follow this railroad past Healey Station. Here you may wish to explore Healey Dell Nature Reserve, if time permits.

6. After the track ends you should follow the road (B6377) through Shawclough when the park is soon reached on your left. The greenhouses are worth a visit. At this point, if you wish to catch the bus home, walk into Rochdale town centre. Leave the park by the same gate as you entered. Cross the road and turn left soon after the school. At the bottom of the hill bear right and cross the bridge and pass in front of the huge factory complex on your right. Turn right down the side of the factory and cross the car park to join a narrow road with a river on your left. You follow this as it ascends and descends, then passes through industrial buildings.

8. Look out for the footpath sign by a row of cottages. Take this path left as indicated. Cross the bridge and follow the path uphill to a stile, with a stream on your right. A little further on you cross the stream and ascend a steep hill which gradually levels and follows a fence on the left. Turn left to pass a far and follow the track to Catley Lane Head.

9. From here you commence the long climb over Rooley Moor Road. In places the paving is still in remarkably good condition. You follow this road for 3 miles to the summit. As you pant your way up spare a thought for the poor packhorses, fully laden with cotton, having to journey to Rawtenstall. If you take a short detour left at the very summit you will see the Triangulation Station, the highest point in Rossendale at 1,555 feet (474m) above sea level. Descend along the stoney track high above Cowpe Reservoir, to the stile on the right of a gate, and continue down the steep track by the breakers' yard. At the junction turn right and follow the lane past recently reclaimed land on the right down to Stacksteads. The car park at which you set out is about one hundred yards up the road to your right.

Near Cloughfoot

WALK 8

IRON BRIDGE - COWPE - LENCH

4 miles

This is a short ramble which provides views over Waterfoot and the peaceful Cowpe Valley. It can be done along with Walk 9 to make a total of 7½ miles for those who prefer a longer ramble.

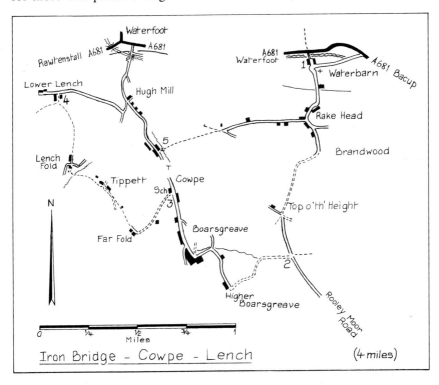

Iron Bridge - Cowpe - Lench   (4 miles)

1. Iron Bridge is half way between Glen Top and Stacksteads, and your car may be parked on the main A681 near to the Iron Bridge, or in the streets by Waterbarn Chapel. From the main road you cross the River Irwell by the Iron Bridge down the side of the shop opposite the bus stop.

Ascend Rake Head Lane past the 1847 Baptist chapel and across the line of the Bacup to Rawtenstall railway, built around 1850.

Climb the steep hill to **Rake Head** and continue straight up between the breaker's yard and the tip entrance. The track steepens, so stop at intervals to rest and enjoy the view to your rear. Go on up, passing between the aerials and Top o'th' Height Farm. At the gate look back down the lane, as on a clear day you will see Pendle Hill summit some 15 miles away.

2. Turn right down the track by a young stream. The original track you have left continues over Rooley Moor to Rochdale and was once used to bring cotton from Manchester. After the next gate the track meanders downhill to Higher Boarsgreave, where you bear right and join a tarmac road descending steeply to the valley bottom by Kearns dyeing mill. Turn right by the mill gate and follow the road past the children's playground, then turn left up a lane signposted to Far Fold Farm.

3. Pass a renovated house and in front of the farm. Your path is between stone gate posts then the wooden stile ahead, keeping the wall on your right. Leave the wall to rise behind the barn to a track joining from the hilltop and descend to Tippet Farmhouse ahead. Cross the stile to go behind a second house, then bear left to follow a fence on your right. This takes you to a stile, a little bridge and a kissing gate. Now follow the railings to rise to a tiny field. Stones mark the way to a stable, then right to another kissing gate. Cross the lane and pass in front of the garages below the large house at Lench Fold. Your exit is by a kissing gate to a green path between walls. Take the lower path to ascend to Lower Lench, where a stile allows entry to a Square. (If you wish to lengthen the walk to 7½ miles you should now read from walk 9, point 2 to the finish, then continue from point one return to here).

4. Turn right to go down to a stone track and turn left at the bottom, then right at Cowpe Road. Care is needed as there is no pavement round the bends.

5. Opposite the Buck Inn take the path left over a bridge and up the side of the field to a gap at the top right hand corner. Go forward, keeping the wall to your right, and at the gate take the lower lane ahead. This is Rake Head Road and will take you to Rake Head, where you turn left to descend to Iron Bridge.

Waterfoot

WATERFOOT - LENCH - RAWTENSTALL

3½ miles - 2½ hours

This is a short walk showing several of the valleys of the Royal Forest of Rossendale, an ancient deer hunting ground.

A suitable car park lies just off the main road on entering Waterfoot from Rawtenstall. Turn off opposite J.A. Taylor's Warth Garage, into Stansfield Road, and turn right at the end to enter the car park.

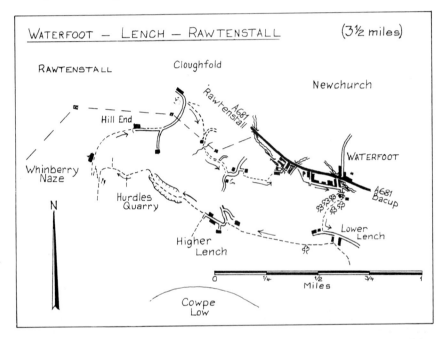

1. The walk starts by following the cobbled street aside the high wall of the railway embankment. This railway came in 1846 as far as Waterfoot, but the terminus was known as Newchurch Station for some time. Before you reach the garages ahead you may wish to take the narrow cobbled street on the left, to the shops for sweets or other provisions. Toilets are available along Burnley Road East a little, and off right by the bus turn-round. Retrace your steps to the garages and turn right to go beneath the railway arch and pass by the cottage. The path now presents a leafy climb to a field and gate near Lower Lench farm.

Turn left at the track and then right into the hamlet square. (You may lengthen this walk to 7½ miles by now following Walk 8 from point 4, until Rakehead; then read from near point 1, Rakehead).

2. Cross the stile at the far end of the square and climb in a 2 o'clock direction towards the trees. This path levels off and continues for a while at the same contour. After crossing a fence without a stile continue towards the house ahead and you will see a stile leading to a metal gate. Your path may be a bit damp just here, so pick your way carefully over the stones and up to a lane. The view over Waterfoot shows The Thrutch glen, which once marked the boundary between the old boroughs of Bacup and Rawtenstall.

3. Turn left and ascend between the houses at Higher Lench to take a stone-slab road leading into an old quarry. On emerging your view is upon Cloughfold, and the track now bears left away from the valley. Climb through the large gate and continue up to the 'crossroads' among the quarry spoil heaps. You should be able to see a distant stile of steps in the wall at a direction of 2 o'clock through a cutting. Proceed to cross this stile and follow a cutting bearing round to the left.

A completely new view is now before you over Rawtenstall to Ski Rossendale opposite. Crawshawbooth and Pendle summit are to your right, while Helmshore, Musbury Tor and the Grane Valley are to your left.

4. When you are ready to leave this kingly castle descend the zig-zag path and pass by the rear of the farm at Whinberry Naze. Follow the wall on your left until you reach a stile. Here you are again above Cloughfold, but now at closer quarters. Across the valley is Marl Pits Sports Centre.

Descend past the farmhouse below and onwards to follow a stone-slab wall on your right. Apparently these large stones were often carried from the quarry on a man's back. Manpower was cheap and livestock expensive.

Waterfoot

5. Before reaching the cottages, take a little gate on the right and follow the higher path around the hillock. The concrete structure below is all that remains of a gas holder, of which there once were four in Cloughfold serving the entire valley.

Join the lane and pass on the left side of the farmhouse under the pylons. Turn down to the stream and cross by the stepping-stones to follow the green unfenced track opposite. Go straight on near the broken wall over the crest of the hillock, and then down to join a farm track.

6. Turn left and descend to enter the farmyard on the right. Enter a field by a gate on your right, then drop down to the gate to your left at the bottom of the field.

The path is now quite apparent, passing a spring and then by a line of hawthornes down to an old building. Here you will find a road which crosses the River Irwell and goes under the railway track to arrive at the main road. Turn right to return to the car park.

WALK 10   O/S 103
SEAT NAZE STROLL
4½ miles - 3 hrs. (damp underfoot in places)

This is a short walk, suitable for an afternoon or summer evening stroll. Park in Waterfoot and walk up Burnley Road East until the wood begins on the left.

1. You will find steps up to a path climbing to the village of Newchurch-in-Rossendale. At the top of the path, on the right, are ruins of the old National School, built in 1829 at a cost of £800. Continue ahead to pass St. Nicholas and St. Johns Church, where an earlier church was founded in 1511. In the churchyard there is a heavy wooden cross, which, until recently, was carried to the top of Seat Naze, a local calvary, thus allowing it to be seen for miles around between Easter and Ascension Day.

2. Continue up to the road junction by the Boars Head and cross to a track between Naze Road and Naze Court. The track takes you to a stile and then open country, where your path climbs to the plateau, with fine views to the east towards Bacup. After a stile your path is fenced and begins to descend. Cross a track and continue down to another track, where you turn right to descend to a bridge.

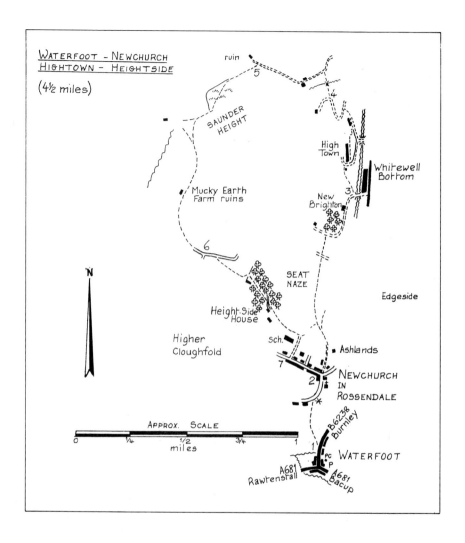

WATERFOOT - NEWCHURCH
HIGHTOWN - HEIGHTSIDE

(4½ miles)

ruin

5

SAUNDER HEIGHT

High Town

Whitewell Bottom

Mucky Earth Farm ruins

New Brighton

3

6

SEAT NAZE

Edgeside

Height-Side House

Higher Cloughfold

Sch.

Ashlands

7

NEWCHURCH IN ROSSENDALE

2

N

APPROX. SCALE

0   ¼   ½   ¾   1
miles

B6238 Burnley

1

WATERFOOT

A681 Rawtenstall

A681 Bacup

3. On your left you will see a steep path above the river. This takes you to a derelict shed, then to a long row of terraced dwellings. Here you should climb the steps at the front of the houses to view the pretty gardens, and then descend steps at the far end to a track. Turn left to ascend again to pass another high-level terrace of houses and a path will bring you to a farm track. Turn left and follow this farm track around a sharp bend to the right.

4. At the next bend keep to the fence on your right to arrive at a gap in the wall. Cross the little stream and continue to the farm track ahead. Turn left to ascend the track, passing a farmhouse and a sawmill.

5. The track eventually arrives at a derelict building, but you should make a left turn after the gateway and follow the gulley up and over the hill, which brings you to a rather boggy field. Your path is across to the far corner, to a rickety stile in a wire fence and a path descending by a wall on your right to a stile and gate. Continue to bear round to your left, passing Mucky Earth ruin until you reach a stile onto a cobbled track joining a tarmac road.

6. Bear left at the junction to ascend for a short while to a stile leading to a field on your right, by a gate. Your path is by an ancient wall on your right towards a derelict building where the path ascends to a stile in the wall. Here you are entering the estate of Height Side, occupied as a Conference and Administration Centre for the European Christian Mission since 1948. The house has a recording studio for broadcasts on Transworld Radio, transmitted from Monte Carlo. There is also a print shop in the grounds. By the house take the upper path to a stile, leaving the woods. Keep the fence on the right and descend to a stile giving access to a road passing the primary school.

7. At the main road turn left and return to the Boars Head, and retrace your earlier route down the path to Waterfoot.

PLEASE OBSERVE THE COUNTRY CODE

Enjoy the countryside and respect its life and work.
Guard against all risk of fire.
Fasten all gates.
Keep your dogs under control.
Keep to public paths across farmland.
Use gates and stiles to cross fences, hedges and walls.
Leave livestock, crops and machinery alone.
Take your litter home.
Help to keep all water clean.
Protect wildlife, plants and trees.
Take special care on country roads.
Make no unnecessary noise.

Notes

Notes

Notes

Notes

Notes

Notes

Notes

Notes